'Visitors to Venice have been recording their impressions and delight in the city over centuries. Gillian Angrave's books show how that appreciation and creativity continues and the Venice in Peril Fund is very grateful to her for supporting its work through the sale of her books.'

Venice in Peril Fund

Other books by Gillian Angrave:

Venice: The Diary of an Awestruck Traveller
(Volume 1: "From Swamp to La Serenissima")
Venice: The Diary of an Awestruck Traveller
(Volume 2: "Betwixt and Between")

"Venice: The Diary of an Awestruck Traveller".

"Pack a copy of this slim, well illustrated book in your pocket as your perfect, personal travel companion for your next trip to Venice".

Vivien Devlin, Guild of Travel Writers

The Smart Leisure Guide, July 2017

"These volumes are an essential read for anyone who wants to immerse themselves in the magic that is Venice. Gillian's style of writing takes you on a journey of discovery that is not merely a guide, but a shared experience of all that is best in this wonderful city. It evokes the happiest of memories for those of us who have been, and the glorious illustrations alone will captivate those who have not yet had the pleasure of seeing the most beautiful city in the world."

Mr and Mrs N Johnson, fellow Venetophiles

Venice: The Diary of an Awestruck Traveller

Volume 3 - Hidden Gems

ANGRAVE Publications

Chichester

First published in Great Britain by ANGRAVE Publications
Copyright © Gillian Angrave 2017

Hardback   ISBN 978-0-9955739-6-3   First Edition
Paperback   ISBN 978-0-9955739-8-7   First Edition

A CIP catalogue record of this book can be obtained from the British Library.
Book designed and typeset by Gillian Angrave
Printed by Imprint Digital.com, Seychelles Farm, Upton Pyne, Exeter, Devon EX55HY
www.gillianangrave.co.uk
info@gillianangrave.co.uk

Front and back covers: Views of Venice from La Campanile di San Giorgio Maggiore

CONTENTS

About the author

Born in Leicester in 1945, Gillian was educated at Guthlaxton Grammar School and the Leicester College of Technology. After 3 years working in Leicester as a PA for an architect, an engineering company and The Rank Organisation, she joined P&O as an Assistant Purser in 1967, sailing in CANBERRA and ORIANA until 1974. After a brief spell ashore, she again got 'itchy feet' and in 1976 joined the Foreign & Commonwealth Office as Ambassador's PA, a position she held (and greatly enjoyed) for 29 years. Her postings took her to the Philippines, Peru, Guatemala, Chile, Mexico and Hungary. Sadly, she had to retire from 'The Office' on 16 April 2005, her 60th birthday.

Single (her love of travel somehow always seemed to get in the way of marriage!), upon retirement Gillian became a Registrar of Marriages in West Sussex, a job she also loves. Now she marries everyone else!

Hobbies: travel; photography; bell-ringing; modern languages; gardening; sport (golf - 1992 Hungarian Ladies Open Champion) - and, of course, writing!

I was born under a meandering star!

For my sister Sheila, with love

Facing page: San Giorgio Maggiore and La Salute

Venice: The Diary of an Awestruck Traveller

Volume 3 — Hidden Gems

By Gillian Angrave

"Live your life like a BUTTERFLY:
Have a rest sometimes, but always remember to FLY"

VOLUME 3 PREFACE

It's not often that people tell you they're exceedingly happy when their affliction is getting worse, but I'm delighted to report that mine has got no better at all — Venetophilia, that is. In fact it's getting really quite bad! And so here I am again, writing Volume 3 of my "Diary of an Awestruck Traveller", in which I look forward to sharing your company as I set out on my fourth and fifth visits to this most magical of cities—Venice.

For me, Venice is studded with hidden gems—of all shapes and sizes! Wherever you go, whichever winding alley you wander down, you will almost certainly discover one tucked away, often not immediately visible, but fascinating and full of interest nonetheless.   This is what draws me time and again to La Serenissima - the search for these little gems!   So, notebook and trusty camera tucked in my still bulging Kipling bag, here I am again, eager to add yet another jewel to this already magnificent crown.   And, as with the first two Volumes, I hope you find what I have written enjoyable, interesting and helpful.

So — time to start meandering together again!

Chapter 1: MY FOURTH VISIT: 17—21 MARCH 2017

Day 1: Friday 17 March 2017

This was to be a visit with a difference.

An advert in the Jules Verne brochure had caught my eye just before Christmas—"Venice from the Water". Just up my street, I thought! I could still do what I wanted to do, but also join any excursions which interested me. Accommodation would be on board the French CroisiEurope "river boat", **Michelangelo** (a boat not a ship as she is not a large sea-going vessel!) which, for me with my love of all things maritime, was an extra bonus. So I set off for Gatwick to catch the 1235 BA flight to Venice full of excitement and anticipation.

I joined our group of ten at the baggage carousel at Marco Polo airport, and imagine my surprise and delight when one of the couples were friends from my posting to Mexico City (1987-91), whom I hadn't seen since then!   This would warrant some serious catching-up to be done at a later date! But first we had to get to the port, so I climbed into one of the two minibuses for our use and set off across the Strada Ponte della Libertà (Causeway) to Venice—the scenic route (cf Volume 2)! The weather was to prove misty most days (not good for photos sadly), but that would never dampen my spirits.

*The mv **MICHELANGELO**, moored at San Basilio on the Canale della Giudecca*

Follow my journey to San Basilio

(my first view of Venice in 2015)

Over the Strada Ponte della Libertà (the Causeway), turn right to the Tronchetto (docks), where a large white liner is moored at the International Maritime Terminal. San Basilio is just behind there!

Of one thing I am absolutely sure. You HAVE to arrive in Venice by water, particularly if this is your first visit! As I say repeatedly, nothing prepares you for your first view of the Canal Grande as you enter it from the Canale di Cannaregio on the Alilaguna water ferry (or private water taxi if you feel like paying €100+ for it). It's just pure magic. Whilst I appreciate that it may sometimes be necessary to take the airport bus (or whatever) to Piazzale Roma, I for one will never go "overland" again. It was an interesting experience to drive over the Strada Ponte della Libertà (Causeway) this once, though disappointing as the view of La Laguna was obscured by mist,cars, trains, lorries etc, so in fact you saw little.   In order to reach San Basilio where the *Michelangelo* was moored, my mini-bus just continued on through the docks at the Tronchetto, past the International Maritime Terminal, until we reached the boat. Not a canal in sight! I could have been any-where!   Still, once the Canale della Giudecca came into view, I began to feel that I was "home" at last!

I do like the **Michelangelo.** She is only 110 metres long, 11.4 metres beam, and has a draft of 1.3 metres, but she is ideal for these Venetian waters. She has 78 cabins, with a maximum passenger capacity of 156. On this trip she was full—we were the only English, but the French were great. It did nothing for my Italian, but my rusty French has improved in leaps and bounds!

I'd paid extra to have a large picture window cabin on the upper deck and this proved a good choice.   I settled in, walked along the quayside to take some misty photos, and then got changed for dinner. As you can imagine, the food was superb!

Towards the end of dinner the *Michelangelo* moved berth. Whilst handy for embarkation,

San Basilio is somewhat out on a limb, far away from the Piazza San Marco. I knew this area quite well as it's near the Chiesa Angelo Raffaele, and it would have suited me as I needed to take more photos around and about. But for others it would be far from ideal. I couldn't resist going "up top" during our passage along the Canale della Giu-decca to take some night shots: it was beautiful. Our destination was the mooring on the

*Sailing by the **ex-Mulino Stucky**, now the Hilton Hotel (see Volume 2), on the Canale della Giudecca, en route to our new mooring at Sette Martiri*

on the Riva dei Schiavoni, next to the Giardini Publicci. This was much better, and we were to stay here until the last afternoon, when the boat would sail back to San Basilio to facilitate disembarkation the next day.

Once in my cabin, I put my feet up for a while and enjoyed a "cuppa". Sadly no little electric kettle this time (safety hazard on board ships —tends to upset the generators, and the Chief Engineer, and blow the electrics). Now I could only get a hot drink from the bar. However, despite this extreme hardship, I survived! The view from my cabin window was super - San Giorgio Maggiore opposite, plus vaporetti sailing very close by *(see photo* — had to remember to keep the curtains closed when dressing!)

Once changed, I headed for the bar and spent a very pleasant evening with our group.

*mv **Michelangelo** (photo Sept 2017) moored at the **Riva dei Sette Martiri**, so named after the shooting that took place there by Germans soldiers of seven partisan political prisoners, taken from cells on San Giorgio Maggiore, on 3 August 1944, as a reprisal and warning to others.*

Day 2: Saturday 18th March 2017

I had my own agenda on our first day. I'd brought a few of my books and flyers with me (now my case really **was** heavy) to show the staff at the Hotel Flora as their hotel was featured. They were thrilled to see what I had written and were most enthusiastic about my new venture. It was good to see them again!

From there I walked to the Campo Santo Stefano, stopping briefly to say hello to a waiter I knew at Le Café, then on to the Ponte dell'Accademia and over the bridge to the Gallerie dell'Accademia which I wanted to visit again to take more photos and get more information. It was still quite early in the morning, so there were few people around and I wandered happily through the Sala in solitary splendour most of the time. Just what I needed. It was good to look at "old friends" again, like Veronese's "Banquet in the House of Levi", but also to study "new" works as in the Jheronimus Bosch exhibition. So I took my photos, found one of the staff who could answer my questions, and thoroughly enjoyed my visit there yet again.

Whilst here, I also found the Anglican Church of St George in the Campo San Vio where I

Top Left: *Walking over the Ponte dell'Accademia to the Gallerie dell'Accademia*

Top Right: *the latest craze in Venice—lovers leave a padlock on the bridges!*

Right: *Leading to the Jheronimus Bosch exhibition*

would attend the Sunday Service on my next visit to Venice in September.

From St George's, it was then a question of taking a back-doubles route along the Calle Lunga down to the Chiese San Sebastiano and Angelo Raffaele again. The former is undergoing renovation of the exterior, so it was difficult to get in, but I enjoyed re-visiting the Angelo Raffaele. This time I was able to take a photo of the beautiful marble shrine dedicated to Tobias and the Archangel Gabriel *(below)* as the church was almost empty.

La Società Bocciofila San Sebastiano

The Custodian of the Angelo Raffaele is a very friendly old gentleman. Unluckily for him, though, he was the one on whom I chose to practise my Italian! I was curious to visit the Bowling Club which I knew was nearby, but I just couldn't find it (apparently bowling was Garibaldi's favourite sport!). As I didn't know the Italian for "bowling", an appropriate action was called for, which the Custodian seemed to find very amusing (this probably explains why I was rubbish at bowling). In the end, though, he got the general idea and pointed me in the right direction. La Società Bocciofila (as I now know a Bowling Club is called) is behind a high wall and iron gates, in an area devoted to allotments and a 1950's (I would guess) small development of flats. You really would never know it was there! Luckily a man was coming out of the gates as I approached. He was delighted to show me the bowling lanes, apologised for having to dash off, but said I could stay for as long as I wanted, which was very kind of him. I doubt whether he gets many foreign visitors!

No-one was playing at the time, so I was able to take a photo. The three indoor lanes looked in very good condition (not that I'm an expert). I don't know how many members there are, but the club seemed to be thriving. I then went outside to look at the allot-

La Società Bocciofila

San Sebastiano

(On the Fondamenta

Briati)

And the allotments next

door

ments. The residents obviously enjoyed being outside and just pottering around chatting to their neighbours. It was a peaceful, happy environment—in stark contrast to the frenetic activity in the tourist parts of Venice—and I was pleased for them.

Making sure I closed the iron gates behind me (as requested), I left La Società Bocciofila, continued a little way along the Fondamenta Briati, then crossed over the Rio dell'Angelo Raffaele onto the Fondamenta del Soccorso en route to the Chiesa Santa Maria dei Carmini, around which is situated the Istituto Superiore d'Arte Applicata (Institute of Technical Industrial Design) covering, from my translation of their syllabus, anything from office furniture, to wi-fi speakers to advertising models etc, worked in metal, ceramics and plastics. As with many other Departments of the Università di Venezia (cf the Palazzo Loredan in the Campo Santo Stefano), every available historic building is used to house them and it is a fitting way of preserving and maintaining these beautiful treasures of architecture.

La Chiesa Santa Maria dei Carmini (The Carmini)

This church, also known as Santa Maria del Carmelo, but generally known as The Carmini, is attached to the former Scuola Grande di Santa Maria del Carmelo or Scuola dei

Carmini (in which part of the Istituto is now housed). Built in the 14th century, it was originally known as Santa Maria Assunta, and its charitable confraternity (Scuola) stemmed from a lay women's association called Le Pinzocchere dei Carmini, founded in 1597. Members of this lay group of women were associated with the neighbouring Carmelite monastery as tertiaries, (members of the Third Order) and were responsible for sewing the Carmelites' Scapulars (short monastic cloaks, with badges of affiliation to a particular Order consisting of two strips of cloth hanging front and back and joined over the shoulders). The Carmini also has a very tall campanile, designed by Giuseppe Sardi, and crowned by a sculpture of the Madonna del Carmine (1982) as a replacement for the original by Romano Vio which was destroyed by lightening. I had wanted to visit The Carmini for a long time, but as I arrived a funeral cortege was about to enter the church, so visitors were not allowed to go in. I shall try to return, though, on my next visit in September.

Not being able to visit the Carmini (I didn't take a photo of the façade out of respect for the funeral party), I then headed off for the next on my list of places to visit today — the Ponte dei Pugni, where I wanted to take a better photo of the bridge and the

*Part of the **Campo di San Barnaba** looking towards the Ponte dei Pugni and the Campanile di Santa Maria del Carmini*

renovated footprints on the bridge (see Volume 1). This done, I sat on a box on the edge of the Rio di San Barnaba and spent a very happy half an hour just day-dreaming and watching the world go by!

By now it was getting on for lunch-time, and I was feeling pretty hungry, so by a very circuitous "andare per le fodere" route (I'm getting good at this!), I made my way to my second favourite restaurant in the Campo Santa Margherita (*right*), where I enjoyed another really fantastic pizza and a welcome glass of wine.

But I hadn't finished my meanderings yet! After lunch it was back down to Ca'Rezzonico to catch the vaporetto to San Marcuola and the Ghetto once more, where I needed another photo of the Shoah (see Volume 2). I love the Ghetto and the Campo del Ghetto Nuovo. I took my photo, lingered a while, and then continued on to La Chiesa Madonna dell'Orto. I didn't go in this time, but strolled along the Fondamenta to the Ospedale Fatebenefratelli and then back the other way to the Sacca della Misericordia, my aim being eventually to get onto the Fondamenta Nuove to visit **I Gesuiti** at last.

It's quite a long, winding route to get there, and by now my legs were beginning to ache, but I was determined to see this church, having been thwarted on my previous

Campo Santa Margherita , *Dorsoduro*

two attempts as it had been closed.

La Chiesa di Santa Maria Assunta detta I Gesuiti (now known as I Gesuiti)

When I went inside this Jesuit church, I was overwhelmed. I just sat quietly - looking, in awe of the sheer beauty. The interior is completely green and white marble, so exquisitely carved that it looks like painted wall-paper. Even the drapery and the tassels on the fringes are marble; and the gold work is beautiful. I'm afraid my photographs don't do it justice. It is truly stunning!

The history of **I Gesuiti** is complicated. The first church on this wetland site is believed to have been paid for by a Pietro [Cleto] Gussoni in 1148, and it was turned into a hospital for poor men and women in 1154. The Gussoni family continued to play an important part in the church's existence until the mid 1600's. In 1523 Sant'Ignazio di Loyola first visited Venice on a pilgrimage to Jerusalem. He returned to I Gesuiti in 1535 with a group of friends calling themselves The Society of Jesus (Jesuits are I Gesuiti in Italian) and they were ordained as priests in this church. Within two years the group had gained a large following throughout La Laguna. They left for Rome in 1537, but in 1606, after quarrels broke out between Pope Paul V and Venice, the city was placed under interdiction and

*La Chiesa Santa Maria Assunta—**I Gesuiti***

I Gesuiti were exiled from Venice until 1657. Between 1606-1657 Venice was also at war with the Ottoman Empire, and a new Pope, Alexander VIII, decided to send the Betlemitani, an Order under his control formed to help the Knights of the Cross and "bolster the troops". In the absence of I Gesuiti, the Betlemitani then took over this church. When they left, Venice sold the whole estate (the church, a hospital and a convent) to I Gesuiti for 50,000 ducats, but this church was now too small for I Gesuiti, so they pulled it down, built their own and named it Santa Maria Assunta. It was designed by Domenico Rossi, who had designed the Chiesa di San Stae; was financed by the noble Manin family, and was consecrated in 1728. The present Pope (2017) Francis is a Jesuit.

It was a difficult task for Rossi as he had to follow strict plans as defined for I Gesuiti by the Council of Trent. The basic design is in the form of a Latin cross with three chapels in the longest wing and six chapels along the nave. There is an impressive pulpit created by Francesco Bonazza, and the most beautiful altar dedicated to the Holy Trinity. The exterior façade is in two tiers, with eight columns on the lower tier supporting the second tier. The square campanile is almost the original one that was built for the Betlemitani. The only addition is the belfry, dating from the 18th century. **I Gesuiti** is so worth a visit.

Below: the stunning gold work enhancing the green and white marble in **I Gesuiti**

(As a slight digression—photos taken on my visit to Rome in May 2017)

*"All roads lead to Rome"! The interior of the **Chiesa del Gesù**, the Mother Church of the Society of Jesus (the Jesuit Order), Via degli Astalli, Rome*

La Chiesa del Gesù, Rome

The tomb of Sant'Ignazio di Loyola, designed by Andrea Pozzo, with its beautiful gold and lapis lazuli pillars, decorations and carvings. In this chapel is the restored **macchina barocca** *(or "conversion machine") by Pozzo. Each day at 17.30, to the accompaniment of loud religious music, the painting slides to one side to reveal for a short time the statue of Sant'Ignazio*

By now it was about 4.15 pm. I was so reluctant to leave the tranquillity and beauty of **I Gesuiti**, but time was marching on and I needed to be back on board the *Michelangelo* for 6 pm in time to get ready for our group's welcome cocktail party at 6.30.

So I hurried back to the Fondamenta Nove to catch the number 52 vaporetto which would take me, via the entrance to the Arsenale and its now deserted shipyards, and Sant'Elena, to the stop at Giardini which was nearest to our boat. Eventually I found the right landing stage (there are quite a few for vaporetti going the other way to the Canale di Cannaregio and to the outer islands) and waited for mine. Not a good idea, though, to travel at rush hour! The vaporetto was packed with Venetians returning home from Murano, Burano, Torcello and Sant'Erasmo, where they had been working during the day, so I spent most of the journey wedged tightly between two workmen, unable to move let alone take a photo of the Armstrong Mitchell crane which was at last visible at the Arsenale. Most people disembarked at Sant'Elena, but as the Giardini was only two stops away, it didn't help much. From what I could see , though, this looked an interesting route and I'll definitely go that way again when it's not so crowded and the weather is clearer.

Once back on board, I got ready and met the others in the bar for a *bellini* cocktail.

A *bellini*, invented sometime between 1934 and 1948 (exact date unknown) by Giuseppe Cipriani, founder of Harry's Bar, which I've been by many times but never in, the Cipriani Hotel and the Locanda Cipriani on Torcello, is a mixture of Prosecco (the preferred sparkling wine: champagne does not go well with the peach) and peach purée or nectar. Prosecco comes from the Italian village of that name near Trieste, and is today produced in nine provinces spanning the Veneto and Friuli Venezia Giulia regions.

Cipriani named it *bellini* because of its unique pink colour which reminded him of the toga of a saint in a 15th century painting by Giovanni Bellini. The cocktail started out as a seasonal speciality at Harry's Bar, a favourite drinking hole of Ernest Hemingway and Orson Welles (I keep illustrious company!) to name but a few, and later became an all year round favourite at Harry's Bar in New York also.

Cocktail and nibbles by my side, I was all set to hear what our group had done, and they wanted to know where I had been, so we had a lot to talk about.   Dinner was served at 7 pm, but our conversations carried on long after that over—yes—more *bellini's*!   As you can imagine, it was a really good evening. Despite the mist, you could see the stars!

The **Michelangelo** at Sette Martiri (view from the Campanile di San Giorgio Maggiore—Sept 2017

Day 3: Sunday 19th March, 2017

Today was "tour day" as I joined our group for a visit to a mask-making workshop and a *squero* (gondola boat yard). We left the **Michelangelo** immediately after breakfast and walked along the Riva dei Schiavoni to catch a vaporetto to Accademia, where we got off and walked through the little back alleys to the mask shop.

The mask-making workshop *(off the Calle Lunga)*

It was a really good quality mask shop, and in the back room the two ladies who run it gave a talk about the history of the masks and the Commedia dell'Arte (which I've written about in Volume 2 , so won't go over again here). However, there are a few interesting points which I didn't cover before or know about.

In the mid-1500's Venetians were living under very strict control. The advent of the Carnival around 1570 and the wearing of masks gave the citizens a freedom which they hadn't known before and enabled them to flaunt the rules, make fun of politicians, and fraternise with people outside their own class. It also enabled citizens to gamble anonymously. However, there was not complete freedom as the Ruling Council had spies

*Wearing the mask and cape of **Il Dottore** (the doctor). This attire in fact pre-dates the Carnival as the doctor needed to be protected at all times from the plague.*

everywhere, and there were still certain rules: you couldn't enter a monastery wearing a mask, nor could you dress like women or carry weapons. But the crime rate invariably soared during Carnivals and the festivities often had to be stopped when things got out of hand.

The mask making workshop:

Filling a mould with papier mâché, and applying gold leaf

There then followed a fascinating demonstration of how the masks are made by filling plaster of Paris moulds with papier mâché, painting them and then applying gold leaf, feathers etc depending on the design. There were some really beautiful masks there and it was tempting to buy one, but as they are quite expensive and you need somewhere at home to show them off to best advantage, which I don't have, I resisted the temptation. Our visit lasted just over an hour and was very informative and enjoyable.

An example of some of the exquisite masks and costumes made in "our" workshop

Il Squero di Tramontin i Figli (Tramontin & Sons)

We then left the workshop and headed to a small café for a quick café latte, before making our way down to the gondola boatyard where, being Sunday, no-one was working. I had thought we would go to the *squero* at San Trovaso, but we went in-stead to the Squero di Tramontin i Figli *(below),* on the Rio Ognissanti (Dorsoduro).

Having written about gondolas in Volume 1, a *squero* was the one place I really wanted to visit to gain a better understanding of the skill involved in making these craft. I learned so much more on this visit. Lengths of wood are chosen that have no knots or white edges; they are carefully stacked horizontally in the open to dry, each centimetre of thickness requiring a year to season; the Veneto foot is used for all measurements as this better suits the gondola's design; the *sercio* (side) is curved using fire on the lower part and water on the upper part; the *corbe* (frames) are crafted first. For the construction, in this *squero* eight (no pine) types of wood are used: oak (solid) for the sides; fir (lightweight) for the bottom; cherry (easy to shape) for the thwarts; larch (lightweight and solid, with good water resistance); walnut (easy to bend) for the frames; linden (stable); mahogany for the superstructure; and elm (flexible) also for the frames.

Since returning home, I've visited the Tramontin website, which is in English and is excellent. The *squero* was founded in 1884 by Domenico Tramontin, having served his apprenticeship in the Casal ai Servi boatyards. He made important changes to the design of the gondolas, which were then adopted by other gondola makers. The *squero's* clients, amongst others, have included the Italian Royal Family, nobility, film stars, other celebritites, the City Police and the Carabinieri.

*Inside the Squero.   Note the **Felze** (cabin) under wraps hanging on the wall at the back*

But what caught my eye most on their website were details of the very important conservation work this *squero* has carried out (and is still doing) on gondolas more than 100 years old. The most prestigious of these is the oldest gondola in the world, built in 1848, which belonged to Robert Browning and is now in The Mariner's Museum in Newport, Virginia. Truly amazing: if you're at all interested in gondolas, this is a great website. It is such a highly skilled art to make them—too much to detail here—and the obvious pride that Signor Tramontin (figli—his father died recently) has for his work and his *squero* was so evident whilst he was explaining it all to us in Italian (he speaks little English—a guide interpreted. I understood parts of what he was saying, but most was too technical for me). It was a joy to see, and I have even more respect for this iconic and stately little craft and the craftsmen who make them than I did before—and I had a lot then.

It was a privilege to be able to visit this gondola boatyard. For me, these unprepossessing workshops are what Venice is about. Skills that have been passed down for generations, and show no signs of being eroded by the advent of motorboats and the like. I hope that Signor Tramontin and his men continue to produce such beautiful craft for many years to come.

*An almost completed gondola, with the **Forcola** lying on its side on the left (the light brown wood)*

I stayed quite a long while at the *squero,* but it was time now to head back to the boat as the **Michelangelo** was going on a short cruise round La Laguna during and after lunch, so I needed to be on board in good time. I made my way back to Accademia via the Zattere and the Rio terà Antonio Foscarini, a walk I love, and caught a vaporetto to Giardini. I was much looking forward to this little cruise, though it was a shame that it was still pretty hazy out there and not much good for photos.

We set sail about 1 pm and the trip lasted just over two hours. I loved it—but then I love any voyage, Laguna, sea—whatever! As I seriously enjoy map and chart reading, before this holiday I had found and treated myself to a set of navigation charts of La Laguna (not cheap!), so I took these "up top" as soon as we left so I could chart our course and locate the landmarks. [My interest in navigation stems from having gained my Steering Certificate (allowing me to steer vessels of more than 12,00 gross registered tonnage) on board ss CANBERRA in 1969. My final test was just after leaving Curacao at night, with tankers at every turn—the QM, though, was always by my side! I was also able to help out on one occasion when the Purser allowed me to do an afternoon 4-8 watch when all the QM's had some sort of virus! You can't hit much mid-Pacific fortunately!]

But I digress.

The crew cast off and we sailed a little way down the Bacino di San Marco until there was sufficient room for a boat of our length to turn round. Slowly we made our way around the eastern tip of Venice (Sant'Elena, with its residential blocks of flats), along the Canal del Marani to La Certosa with its busy yacht marina, and up to the south-east corner of Murano, along the Canale del Ondello. I still couldn't see much as we turned south to follow the Porto di Sant'Erasmo channel and back to Venice via San Nicolo, the most eastern point of Lido, and San Servolo, so no worthwhile photos I'm afraid. It was a great trip, though, and I was glad I had splashed out (so to speak) and bought the charts. I shall look at them often, I know, both for pleasure and for information.

Once back on "terra firma", as the weather was much better now (typical), I collected my things and set off again, this time for the vaporetto to take me to the Ponte di Rialto. There was a building there that I was particularly keen to see — the newly renovated by Benetton—***Fondaco dei Tedeschi***.

Il Fondaco dei Tedeschi, *Rialto, newly refurbished by Benetton*

The new swish interior of the **Fondaco dei Tedeschi**

Il Fondaco dei Tedeschi

It's amazing what money can do!   I'd written quite a lot about this building in Volume 2, and the refurbishment of it by Benetton. Now that it was finished at last (just after Christmas, I think), I was very curious to see what they had done to it. To say the interior is impressive is an understatement. It is lovely, but rather "exclusive", as you can see. The designer boutiques in the galleries sell high quality items, at designer prices, and I gather it's become very popular with well-heeled visitors from the Middle East and Russia in particular.   I enjoyed looking, but didn't buy!

No expense has been spared, and as I had said before, if this is the only way to preserve some of Venice's beautiful buildings, then so be it. But I can understand why Venetians are so against it. For most of them it's out of their reach.

But there is one great feature — the **roof terrace**. This is open to everyone and is free. You have to get a coloured disc which gives you the time of your visit, and each group of 30 or so is only allowed 12 minutes up there to take photos to ensure everyone gets a turn: it's very popular as you can imagine. But 12 minutes is fine. That's all you need. Once up there, the views are stunning, and there are very helpful metal maps showing

*Above: Looking towards the **Scuola Nuova della Misericordia**, with the campanile of **Madonna dell'Orto** in the background*

Views from the Fondaco dei Tedeschi

*Below: Looking towards the campanile of **San Bartolomeo**, built 1747-54 (this became the church of the Tedeschi (German community). The Basilica and the campanile di San Marco are in the distance.*

*From the roof terrace of the **Fondaco dei Tedeschi**: Looking over the **Ponte di Rialto** along the **Canal Grande** (the Rialto vaporetto stop is on the left)*

The imposing **San Zanipolo** *(la Chiesa di Santi Giovanni e Paulo)*
from the **Fondaco dei Tedeschi**

what you are looking at. Once down from the terrace, I had a browse in some of the galleries and then wandered back to the Rialto vaporetto stop. As ever, I loved the journey to San Marco, where I got off and strolled along the Riva dei Schiavoni, savouring the late afternoon weak sun. I had a quick walk down the Via Garibaldi looking for John Cabot's house (no 2), but it must have been demolished as I couldn't find it, and no-one else whom I asked had a clue where it was either. Not that it mattered. For me this has to be one of the most tranquil and beautiful *rio terrà* in Venice. I just enjoyed it!

From here it was only a stone's throw to the Giardini Publicci, where Venetian families were making the most of the light that was still left before returning home. These are such pleasant gardens, and it was lovely to see the children running around freely. I found a park bench and spent a very contented 15 minutes or so just relaxing.

By now it was nearly 5 pm—time to return to the boat and catch up with the group. I much enjoyed hearing of where they had been after the tours, and I was able to tell them about the roof terrace at the Fondaco dei Tedeschi, plus other bits of general information that they were keen to know about. I sampled another *bellini* (well, someone has to do it!) and then continued recounting my stories over yet another delicious dinner. I must say the catering on board was excellent. Having seen our large and complicated galleys on my P&O ships, I'm full of admiration for the crew of the **Michelangelo.** Their galley is in the bow and is tiny in comparison. How they manage to produce such haute cuisine is beyond me. All the crew seem keen and very willing to multi-task too. Even our "purser" (Hotel Manager or whatever they call them these days) helped out in the restaurant *(below).* Hmmm! You wouldn't have seen mine doing

that! But then these are modern times. with different work ethics quite unlike the "good old days" of the 1960's and 70's. Such camaraderie, though, does make for a very "happy ship" which in turn impacts on passengers. I was much impressed.

Day 4: Monday 20th March 2017

As I drew back the curtains at 7 am, my heart sank. Oh no: not another Victor Meldrew "I DON'T BELIEVE IT" day! But it was. I doubt I could see more than 20 feet for the thick fog that was swirling around the **Michelangelo** - an absolute "pea-souper" in fact. This would be interesting. We were due to leave our mooring at Sette Martiri shortly en route to Chioggia, but in this we were going nowhere. Nothing was moving on La Laguna. No familiar chug of the vaporetti's engines, no shouts to mates from one *topo* to another. Absolute silence.   It was so eerie.

So here we stayed until 9.15 am, by which time the fog had cleared sufficiently for our Captain and the pilot to deem it safe to set sail. Sadly I waved goodbye to our berth at Sette Martiri as the **Michelangelo** swung round to head off south-west to our destination.   Again I was "up top" with my charts, but this time I was joined by some of the French contingent who were also keen to see where we were going. It was damp and still misty, so sadly disappointing for photos yet again (but I've done my best!).   My own group preferred to stay below, warm and dry, having an extra cup of coffee.   Sensible lot!

So you can follow our passage to Chioggia past Lido and Pellestrina
(Taken from the International Space Station; grateful thanks again to NASA Earth Science and
Remote Sensing Unit, Johnson Space Center, for letting me use this photograph—again!)

I had to admire our young Captain. It must be really difficult to steer our boat at the best of times. Whilst she is not 'tall', she is very long, and it must be difficult to judge exactly where the stern is. I'm sure one of the Deck Department would be aft, with radio, keeping an eye on things, but our Captain was obviously highly skilled. No worries there!

Passage to Chioggia

On the NASA photograph, you can clearly see Venice and the Causeway; Punta Sabbioni on the right; the first long strip that is Lido, and the second that is Pellestrina; the two Lidi separating them (where the new flood barriers are situated); and part of the Lido di Chioggia at the bottom left hand corner. How I love this view!

From our berth we headed south along the Canale Santo Spirito, passing the islands of San Clemente, Santo Spirito and Poveglia, until we joined the Rochetta di Malamocco channel at Malamocco, near the southern end of Lido. We continued to follow Lido close in-shore until we reached the Batteria della Rochetta (a fort) at the Lido di Malamocco entrance to La Laguna. From there we followed a south-westerly course until we joined the narrow Canale di San Pietro at the tip of Pellestrina.

En route to Chioggia
(a misty journey)

Below: Pellestrina's
answer to the rubbish tip!

Above: a gloomy **Poveglia**
(the "Island of Sadness" -
see Volume 2), with its
octagonal fort in front

The main street of **Pellestrina**, *with the Chiesa di San Antonio di Padova in the background*

Our passage continued along the Canale di Pellestrina, still close in-shore, until we reached the Roman fort Caroman (Ca'Roman) and the small Villaggio of the same name, on the very southern tip of the island This is a protected area of pinewoods and sand dunes renowned for its flora and fauna, and particularly for its birdlife.

Here our channel joined the Canale Taglio Nuovo, coming from the north-west.   At last we reached Chioggia, where we moored safely at the CTC Chioggia Terminal Crociere . In all our journey had taken about an hour and a half, and as ever I had loved every minute of it, despite the lack of sun!

Chioggia

Chioggia lies on the Brenta estuary, with the Brenta river/canal, the Canale dei Cuori, the Canale Gorzone, the Rio Adige and many little tributaries all flowing into it. I had wanted to visit Chioggia for a long time. She is billed as a "second Venice", but I think this is rather unfair to both islands. You imagine grand palazzi, narrow alleyways and winding canals, but Chioggia has none of these. As La Laguna's main fishing port, she is busy, there is traffic, and from what I could see, few buildings of note. She consists principally of two islands, Chioggia and the large resort island of Sottomarina, with many smaller islands dotted around, all inter-linked by bridges and highways.   Chioggia herself is bisected by the Canale Vena. To the north (the La Laguna side), the Canale Lombardo separates her from the actual port and cruise terminal, whilst to the south a small bridge over the Canale San Domenico leads to the Isola dei Cantieri with its market, warehouses and, looking at the map, not much else. Sottomarina lies further south, with a highway connecting her eventually to the mainland. I made the most of my brief time in Chioggia, but I wouldn't go again. On a sunny day and with more time, it may look different. But I doubt it (sorry Chioggia!).   I leave it to you!

54

Chioggia:

The **Municipio** *(town hall)* on the Corso del Popolo, with the **Basilica di San Giacomo**

Because we were late leaving Venice, our time here was shorter than it should have been. It was now almost 11 am, and I had just over an hour to look around before the **Michelangelo** set sail again to return to Venice (but back to San Basilio this time) so the crew could have some well deserved time ashore (I know how precious that is!). As I was on the afternoon tour to Padova, I therefore needed to set off at a smart pace in or-der to explore as much of Chioggia as I could in the time I had, camera as always at the ready!

I walked along part of the Corso del Popolo (main street) and then branched off to the Canale Vena *(opposite):* pleasant — but I missed the palazzi of Venice! Halfway along, I crossed over the Canale and walked to the bridge over the Canale San Domenico, but there was not enough time to go further to the Isola dei Cantieri. Had I but known, I should have gone the other side of the Corso, which was more interesting, I gather. But I didn't. You live and learn!

I made my way back to the Canale della Vena and down to the Piazzetta Vigo at the end. It has a very elegant bridge here (the most beautiful of all the 8 bridges in Chioggia), built in 1685 and enhanced in the 18th century with Istrian marble.

Nearby, the Colonna Vigo stands in the Piazzetta. It was erected in 1786 on the orders of the Mayor, Giulio Antonio Mussato, before the decline of Venice's influence. It is carved from a single piece of white marble, crowned with the Byzantine statue of the Lion of San Marco of Venice. I did like it—delicate yet impressive.

La Colonna Vigo

*The elegant **Ponte Vigo**, at the western end of the Canale Vena*

It was at the Ponte Vigo that for me things seemed to go downhill! Whilst taking a photo of the bridge, I knocked my sunglasses off and one of the lenses fell out. Try as I could, it just wouldn't stay back in. Age, medications etc seem to have given me a type of hay fever, and made my eyes much more light sensitive (no fun getting old!). So even though the sun wasn't shining, I knew this wouldn't be good news, and it wasn't! Within about 15 minutes my eyes were streaming, they stung like mad, and had begun to close up. I struggled with the lens again. No luck. I even went into the nearest shop to seek help, but the shopkeeper couldn't fix it either. By this time I was having trouble seeing where I was going, but I soldiered on (bravely, I thought) as time was running out and I had to be back with the group at noon. I stumbled along the Corso del Popolo, bumping into people on the way, determined to take what photos I could (but they were rubbish), until I reached the Torre di Santa Maria where I was to board the coach for Padova. Everyone was rather concerned to see me in such a distressed state, but a group effort managed to get the lens to stay back in. Was I grateful. Thanks everyone!

 Now, with my sunglasses back on, things quickly started to improve. Such a relief—I had visions of having to stay on the bus and not seeing anything of Pàdova.

Chioggia:

Above: *the* **Porta di Santa Maria** *, with its Lion of San Marco*

Above right: *the* **Corso del Popolo** *(the main street)*

Right: *along the* **Canale Vena** *(with the Basilica di San Giacomo in the distance)*

Above: the ***Canale Vena***

(no gondolas here!)

Right:

Cattedrale San Martino

Pàdova (Padua)

The coach arrived at the Torre at about 12.30 pm and I, plus six of our group and a small French contingent from our boat, climbed on board and headed out to the Veneto and our ultimate destination of Pàdova.

Many books have been written about this historic university city, so I will only touch briefly on its history and the main points of interest.

Pàdova (its correct Italian name: the name Padua is of German origin), is situated on the Venetian Plain (Pianura Veneta) (Veneto) and stands on the Rio Bacchiglione , which used to surround it like a moat. It is 25 miles (40 kms) west of Venice and 18 miles (29 kms) south-east of Vicenza. The Rio Brenta, which used to run through it, still flows through the northern districts . It is the seat of the famous University of Pàdova, founded in 1222, where Galileo Galilei was a lecturer. It is also the setting for Shakespeare's "Taming of the Shrew", and Oscar Wilde's "The Duchess of Padua".

In 2011 its population numbered 214,000, but the city, along with Venice, is often included in the Pàdova-Treviso-Venice Metropolitan Area, which has a population of around 1,600,000.

Pàdova claims to be the oldest city in northern Italy, being founded around 1183 BC by the Trojan prince, Antenor. After the Fall of Troy, Antenor teamed up with the Veneti (who had lost their King) and moved to the Euganean Plain, now the Veneto. Various tribes (Etruscans, Gauls, Spartans) tried to conquer them, but were defeated by the Veneti, now the predominant tribe in the Veneto. The Veneti then formed an alliance with Rome in 226 BC against their common enemy, the Gauls, and later the Carthaginians, and Pàdova gradually became part of the Roman Republic.

Centuries later the citizens of Pàdova, like the original Venetians, were constantly being attacked by the marauding Huns, Lombards and Goths, and were forced to flee to La Laguna and the surrounding hills when their city was burned to the ground by the Lombards. Some citizens returned, but the city never totally recovered. It came under the rule of Venice in 1405, and stayed so (mostly) until the Venetian Republic fell in 1797 after the invasion of Napoleon. In the succeeding years its history was chequered. It suffered greatly during World War I, and was bombed extensively during World War II, finally being liberated on 25 April 1945 by partisans and troops of the British Eighth Army. There is a small Commonwealth War Graves Cemetery in the western part of the city.

*The beautiful **Prato della Valle**, Pàdova's principle square since Roman times*

After the War, Pàdova developed rapidly, as with the rest of the Veneto, and is today one of the most prosperous and active regions of modern Italy.

Our tour of Pàdova

It took about an hour or so to arrive at this historic city. I had wanted to drive through the Veneto to get an idea of what this region was like, having read so much about it. It is, of course, a flat coastal plain, but it was pleasant and there were some pretty villages from what I could see, though we travelled along the main highway most of the way.

Once in Pàdova, the coach dropped us off at the elegant and impressive **Prato della Valle** (*Prà dela Vale* in Venetian), the main square of the city. Covering 90,000 square metres, this is the largest square in Italy and one of the largest in Europe.

Today there is a large green space in its centre, *l'Isola Memmia*, which is surrounded by a small canal bordered by two rings of 78 (originally 88) statues (40 on the outer ring, 38 on the inner ring). These were sculpted in stone from Vicenza between 1775 and 1883 by different artists, and represent various famous Venetians, Romans, "celebrities of the time", and Doges (though most of the latter were destroyed by Napoleon in 1797). One such beautiful statue is dedicated to Andrea Memmo (1729-93), noted diplomat

*One of the four elegant bridges in the **Prato della Valle**, with statues of Andrea Mantegna and Pope Paul II, Bishop of Pàdova, on the outer ring, and Umberto Pallavicino and Pietro Ottoboni inside*

(Ambassador to Constantinople), scholar, politician, and member of one of the oldest Catholic families in Venice (Pisani). I was unaware of this at the time, so no photo I fear.

During the Roman period, The **Prato** was a vast theatre arena with a semi-circular Roman orchestra pit. In 1077 it became a cattle market (a modern cattle market was held here from 1913 to 1968), and the location for two large fairs in October and November each year. In 1257 it also became the venue for the newly instituted "Palio del Santo", held on 20 June for many years hence to celebrate Pàdova's freedom from the tyrannical rule of Ezzelino. There were chariot races, jousting contests, side shows and stalls etc. It then fell into decay and by the middle of the 18th century, when Venice no longer owned it, and the Abbey of Santa Giustina could no longer afford to look after it, it had become an abandoned swampy marsh. In 1767 the Senate decided it was to become public property, and the Venetian Procurator, Andrea Memmo, wasted no time in reclaiming it and re-designing it as it is today. During the 1990's it again became neglected, much to the consternation of the citizens of Pàdova who, with help, have now restored it to its former glory. A credit to them. It really is lovely.

From the Prato you can see the **Basilica del Sant'Antonio** (Basilica of St Anthony of Pàdova) and it wasn't far to walk there for the next stop on our itinerary.

La Basilica del Sant'Antonio (La Basilica del Santo)

St Anthony was born in Lisbon and only lived in Pàdova for a short time. He preached tirelessly, was very charismatic, and his Sermons drew in large crowds (his Lenten Sermon in 1231 attracted 30,000). This Sermon was to be his last, though, as he died whilst travelling on June 13, 1231, at the age of 40, in the Franciscan Convent of Santa Maria della Cella, annexed to the Convent of the Poor Clares. After his death a bitter dispute broke out between the Poor Clares nuns and the Franciscans about where his remains should lie — where he had died, or the Franciscan Convent of Santa Maria Mater Domini, where he had lived. Eventually he was buried in the Franciscan Convent, and construction began to build a much more fitting resting place—the present Basilica - (1232-56), which would incorporate the Maria Mater Domini Convent. This Convent is known today as the Cappella della Madonna Mora. Relics of St Anthony (his tongue and chin) lie in the Treasury Chapel, but his body rests in a separate side chapel, the Chapel of the Ark of St Anthony.

It is a beautiful church, full of exquisite treasures, works of art and religious artefacts. I loved the Cloisters too. You cannot be in Padova and not visit **La Basilica**. It's a must!

La Basilica del Sant'Antonio, *Pàdova, the Byzantine domes mirroring those of San Marco in Venice*

The central nave of the **Basilica del Sant'Antonio**

La Basilica del Sant'Antonio di Pàdova

Above*: The **Treasury Chapel**, with the Reliquary of the Tongue in the centre*

Above Right: *The **Ark of Saint Anthony***

Below Right: *The **Convent cloisters***

La Piazza delle Erbe
Il Palazzo della Ragione

Built in 1218-19 as a much lower structure, it was the Municipal Palace housing the court, offices of the "Cataveri" (the Inquisition) and a jail. Today it is one of the most important public buildings from mediaeval times.

After leaving the Basilica, I made my way through winding streets, past part of the University and the Town Hall, till I came to the Palazzo della Ragione in the Piazza delle Erbe. Sadly, there wasn't much time to linger here, nor have a coffee in the famous Café Pedrocchi nearby (akin to Florian's in Venice), so I made my way back down the Via Roma to the Prato to wait for our bus. I just managed a quick look inside the Basilica di Santa Giustina (somewhat austere) before the bus arrived to take us back to the **Michelangelo** at San Basilio. A pleasant ride in the evening sunshine. Even the Ponte della Libertà looked vaguely inviting — but not that much!

Once back on board, time again for another catch-up with the group before making my way to the restaurant for the Gala Night. It was a great evening, the food was fantastic and I felt sad that yet another stay in my favourite "water city" was coming to an end.   I went back to my cabin to pack (cases out by 8 am), sort through my photos - and flop!   It had been another long and busy day, but I had enjoyed every minute of it (even the eyes, now fine, were a distant memory!).

Day 5: Tuesday 21st March 2017

Our two minibuses came at 9 am take us to Marco Polo Airport. Back over the Causeway again (groan!) and along the autostrada to the airport.   I took one last, wistful look at La Laguna, but knew that I would be back in September for a week, so leaving didn't seem quite so bad. It was a good flight back, I said my goodbyes to the group and was back home in no time. A visit with a difference this time, but it only reinforced my love affair with Venice even more. Don't worry, though. As I always say**,**

I shall return!   Ciao Venezia—fino a Settembre

A tranquil Canal Grande

Chapter 2: MY FIFTH VISIT: 22-28 September 2017

And so I did!   I just can't seem to stay away.

A lot had happened since my last visit in March. Sales of Volumes 1 and 2 of my books on Venice were steady, though I still needed that "lucky break" in a very competitive market.   I had had articles published in various magazines; encouraging reviews; I had given talks on radio programmes and been out and about speaking to various societies (Rotary, Mothers Union etc).   I had joined a Literary Society and an independent authors/self publishing group. I had also mastered, more or less, Powerpoint presentations (amazing)! And whilst producing a book yourself is really hard work, full of pitfalls, a steep learning curve and would seem to involve taking out a long-term lease with the church mice, I felt at last I was "getting there" (where, I'm not sure, but there somewhere)!   More than anything, I wanted my books to inspire others to undertake their own meanderings and learn more of this magical city.   I hoped my enthusiasm was catching on, if not quite paying off as yet.

The frescoed map of Venice in the Gallery of Maps, Vatican Museum, Rome. *One of a series of 40 topographical maps of Italy based on drawings by friar and geographer, Ignazio Danti. Commissioned by Pope Gregory XIII in 1580, it took Danti 3 years (1580-1583) to complete the 40 panels. (Photograph taken by me on my second visit to Rome in May 2017)*

Day 1: Friday 22 September 2017

And so began my fifth visit to my "dream islands". I set out to fly from Gatwick on Easyjet at 1230 on Friday 22nd September 2017!

I'd decided to return to the Albergo Bel Sito e Berlino (now called Hotel Bel Sito) in the Campo Santa Maria del Giglio. I do like this hotel and it's only a short walk from the Giglio vaporetto stop down the tiny Calle Gritti, important with my, as ever, heavy suitcase (not only did I have my little electric kettle, tea bags etc: now I had weighty books as well!). I was also nursing a painful right shoulder (sustained whilst bell-ringing), and bursitis of the left hip joint (sustained who knows how), but I was de-termined that these were not going to spoil my visit.

As previously, I'd already booked my vaporetto and Alilaguna tickets on-line through Venezia Unica (reeling at the shock of the increased price because of the exchange rate (€60 for a 7-day vaporetto pass, €27 for an Alilaguna return), so once at Marco Polo airport, after a good flight, I exchanged my vouchers for tickets and headed off to the new Alilaguna and water taxi terminal.

Inside the new Alilaguna and water taxi terminal.

A vast improvement—organized, and with much easier landing stages (also with loos!). The former outside landing stages are to the right

I must say I was very impressed. You still have to go a fair distance to reach the landing stages (adjacent to the old outside ones), but this time it's along moving walkways with colourful murals one side and glass windows the other. The terminal is spacious and well organised, with a café at the far end and, wonder of wonders, loos!   Of course my landing stage would be at the far end (number 13), but it wasn't that far. However, my heart sank when I saw the queue. Quite a few planes had arrived at the same time, so it would seem, and in the end I had to wait (standing) for an hour and a half to get on my Linea Arancio ferry to Giglio.   Not a good start!

But all was forgotten once we set off, bouncing along a choppy La Laguna, and I was glad to be of help (asked for) to a couple visiting Venice for the first time. It was worth the journey just to see their faces as we turned into the Canal Grande! And I, too, was so happy to be back.

I got off at Giglio and made my way to the Bel Sito. The staff there remembered me (amazingly) from my previous stay, and we had quite a chat about my books, proposed itinerary during the next 6 days etc. I settled into my very pleasant single room on the third floor facing the Chiesa Santa Maria del Giglio, and then, as it was by now quite late

The Hotel Bel Sito,

Campo Santa Maria del Giglio

The elegant interior of the **Hotel Bel Sito.** Part of the lounge, looking towards the dining area

Next page:

The very pleasant, tranquil

courtyard

and I was pretty tired, I headed for (yes, you've guessed it) Le Café in Campo Santo Stefano (or to give it its formal name—Campo Francesco Moresini) for a welcome dinner.

Le Café

Why do I always go back to Le Café when there are so many other fine restaurants in Venice? Eating out in the evenings as a single female isn't always that easy. You feel you stand out like a sore thumb and, as I've found, you're not that welcome in smaller, more intimate restaurants or trattorie as you take up a table for two (or even four) and it's bad for business! During the day it's quite easy, but at night it's different. I've tried a few other restaurants, but have been disappointed with the service and, in one case, the food. Also, after a really tiring day, as mine usually is as I try to pack as much as I can into it, I really don't have the energy nor inclination to go that far.

At Le Café I'm now known and much welcomed! The staff are great: courteous, helpful and good humoured. It's not too far from the Bel Sito, the prices are reasonable, and the food is excellent. I feel comfortable eating here, so apologies if I seem boringly predictable and unadventurous, but Le Café it is!

***Le Café, Campo
Santo Stefano***

Below:

*Just opened: a quiet
moment at the begin-
ning of a busy day*

Il Museo della Musica, San Maurizio.

Contrabasso: *Left (Scuola Bresciana), 1650; middle (Nicolo Amati, Scuola Cremona—Antonio Stradivari was apprenticed to Amati 1656-8) 1670; right (Michelangelo Bergonzi, Scuola Cremona) 1755.*

La Musica

Venice is renowned for her music (La Fenice Opera House, Vivaldi to name but two examples). She was in fact one of the European capitals of music, especially in the 18th century when theatres here, particularly during the Carnivale, were the venues for great concerts, attended not only by Venetians but also by many European visitors, particularly those undertaking the Grand Tour.

One of the little gems I discovered en route to Le Café is the Museo della Musica in the deconsecrated Chiesa di San Maurizio (Campo San Maurizio). My sister Sheila, a flautist, found it first and loves it. The original church was founded before 1000, but was rebuilt several times over the centuries until its final reconstruction in 1806 to a design by La Fenice's architect, Giannantonio Selva. It once housed the studio of a young Antonio Canova. Entry is free, and you are greeted with beautiful background music as you step inside. This museum is mainly dedicated to violin making, for which Venice was famous, and focuses on music of Baroque Venice.   There is a wonderful collection of well preserved instruments: mainly violins, cellos and lutes, but there are also wind instruments (flutes etc—I particularly love the "fagotto", which Sheila tells me is an early bassoon) as well as harps and mandolins. There is a little violin workshop, but it was closed when I visited. I loved to stop off here each time I came this way—a true gem! And if you're lucky, you may even get to attend one of the concerts here, though sadly I didn't.

Left: *San Maurizio*

Right: *Selection of violins*

Left: *Il Fagotto*

Right: *More information and displays*

Not far from San Maurizio, in a small campo tucked away at the left corner of Campo Santo Stefano, is the imposing Venice Conservatory of Music *(below left)*, from which echoed forth the strains of much practising of scales. And on the opposite side of the Campo Santo Stefano, en route to the Ponte dell'Accademia, is the ex-Chiesa di San Vidal *(below right)* where concerts are frequently held.

Inside the ex-Chiesa di San Vidal

(note the red fabric round the pillars, quite common in Venetian chiese)

Saturday 23rd September, 2017

I opened the shutters to a cloudless blue sky. A hot and sunny day to come, so the forecast said. Brilliant! Good for meandering and taking lot of photos. So after an excellent breakfast, I decided today I'd dedicate the morning to — books!

I Libri

In Volume 1, I retraced the steps of Julia Garnet in Salley Vickers' excellent book "Miss Garnet's Angel". So, continuing in a "literary vein", this trip I had decided to follow in the footsteps of Commissario (Commissioner) Guido Brunetti and his Inspector Vianello, much loved characters in Donna Leon's popular detective books set in Venice. As well as the plots, I love the insight one gets into the Venetian character, and the interesting snippets of information (which I find useful for my books). Armed with my map, I love to curl up with her books and follow Brunetti as he walks around Venice in his hunt for criminals.

This trip, as I would be doing a tour of La Fenice, I was reading "Death at La Fenice", and as I had also read "A Sea of Troubles", I was keen to visit Pellestrina.

*An iconic and atmos-pheric winter image from the 1970's showing two **Carabinieri**, capes flowing, crossing the Piazzetta di San Marco*

(They ceased to wear these uniforms in the 1990s, I believe)

(photo courtesy F.G.B)

I love this photo!

As Brunetti's HQ is La Questura on the Fondamenta di San Lorenzo, and his office looks out on La Chiesa di San Lorenzo, I thought I'd improve my knowledge of Castello by going to look for them. Easier said than done! I should have paid more attention to the routes he took! I set off along the Riva dei Schiavoni and turned up the Calle della Dose towards the leaning Campanile of San Giorgio dei Greci. So far so good, but then I got very lost, turned down many dead ends and even walked by La Questura twice before realising where I was! I thought the HQ would be a large building, like the one where the police launches are moored on the Canale di Santa Chiara, but not so, as you can see. This me-ander turned out to be a "tour de force". Joe Links would have been proud of me! By the time I found the HQ I was getting very short on patience; my hip was killing me; and I was sick of bridges! But if I set my mind to something, I get on and do it, and at least now I can visualise where Brunetti and his egotistical Sicilian Vice-Questore, Patta, hang out. How I envy Venetians as they navigate these tiny alleyways with ease. No wonder crime in Venice on the whole is low. Unless you are a native, you have little hope of find-ing your way out of the maze when trying to escape!

La Questura,

Fondamenta di San Lorenzo

Commissario Brunetti's place of work. Patta's office no doubt has the curtains!

(Read the books!)

La Chiesa di San Lorenzo

(at present undergoing renovation) onto which Brunetti's office looks

Still on my "book quest", my next stop was to be the Libreria Alta Acqua on the Calle Lunga Santa Maria Formosa, just off the Campo Santa Maria Formosa. I looked at my map with a certain amount of despair as it seemed a long and complicated walk to get there. But I trudged on stoically and eventually arrived with not too much problem. I needed a sit down and so sought sanctuary in the lovely Chiesa di Santa Maria Formosa. But a wedding was just about to take place and the guests had already gathered, so no chance to linger there. When I told one of the Ushers that I conducted civil

wedding ceremonies, he graciously invited me to stay till the bride arrived, which I did. I have to say she looked stunning on the arm of her very proud father. I've rarely seen such a beautiful bride!

"May your hands always be clasped in friendship, and your hearts forever joined in love".

Libreria Alta Acqua

But onwards and upwards: I still had to get to Alta Acqua. I found it fairly easily and what a gem it is!   I couldn't believe my eyes. I was mesmerized. How do they find anything in there?   I gave my card and flyer to a gentleman whom I took to be the owner, who liked the look of my books and said he'd buy both sets, so I promised to return with them later.

Seek, and thou shalt find - maybe!

How DO they find anything in this place?

Don't think I'll ever be this prolific!

Even the steps are books—a bit rickety, though!

Now where exactly IS "The Owl and the Pussycat"? It must be here somewhere!

I could have stayed all morning at Alta Acqua, but by now I was ready for something to eat, and so found a pizzeria in the Campo Santa Maria Formosa. Was I glad of a sit down! I had a beer and a toasted sandwich and chatted to a very pleasant English couple on the next table. They didn't know of Alta Acqua, so I pointed them in the right direction and off they went.

What to do next? I decided to walk to San Zanipolo and then on to the Fdta Nove to catch a vaporetto at Ospedale to take me via San Zaccaria to La Giudecca. I do like this route round Sant'Elena, passed the Giardini Publicci (busy at it was the Biennale), and then the Arsenale, where I got another look at VIPF's Armstrong Mitchell crane there. Eventually I got off at Zitelle on La Giudecca and walked along the Fdta delle Zitelle till I found another peaceful café overlooking the Dogana. Time for my first well-earned gelato of this trip and a cold drink, so I spent a very leisurely half hour just watching the river traffic go by as I devoured an enormous cornetto. Did I feel guilty? Not a bit! As it was a beautiful afternoon, still quite hot, and only 4 o'clock, I felt now would be a good time to go up the Campanile di San Giorgio Maggiore. The sun was in the right direction for some good photos, so I caught a vaporetto at Zitelle to San Giorgio, which

My café on the
Fondamenta delle
Zitelle, La
Giudecca

(with the Campanile
di San Giorgio
Maggiore in the
background)

was the next stop and only took a mere five minutes or so.

San Giorgio Maggiore and La Campanile

I do love this island, with its yacht marina and superb views of the Palazzo Ducale and San Marco and all along the Riva dei Schiavoni to the Giardini.   It's never crowded and I like nothing more than to perch on a bollard and enjoy the peace and quiet. Built between 1566-1610, this Benedictine Church and monastery are amongst Palladio's finest designs. The interior is not ornate, but there are some important works by Tintoretto, one (his last work in the Chapel of the Dead) finished by his son, Dominico.

La Chiesa di San Giorgio Maggiore

*The interior of **San Giorgio Maggiore**, with a Biennale exhibit in the centre*

102

*On **San Giorgio Maggiore**. My "old friend" the western Instrian stone lighthouse (from Volume 2), with the Campanile di San Marco in the backgound.*

The Bacino
(yacht basin) di
San Giorgio
Maggiore

My main reason for visiting the island this time, though, was to go up the Campanile from where, I gathered, the views are beautiful. First built in 1467, the Campanile collapsed in 1774. It was subsequently rebuilt in the neo-classical style and finished by 1791. It took a bit of time finding out exactly where to go up it. It's not at all obvious, but the small passageway to the ticket desk and lift is tucked away at the left corner of the church just before the altar. There was no queue, and the views are stunning, as I hope you agree!

The Campanile and Piazza di San Marco, and Palazzo Ducale

Rio dei Greci*: leaning Campanile and dome of San Giorgio dei Greci; San Lorenzo (scaffolded)*

The Monastery gardens, maze and part of the Convention Centre

Monastery and Cloisters of San Giorgio Maggiore. **Background:** *Hotel Cipriani with pool, La Giu-decca (Italian navy frigates); islands of San Clemente, Sacca Sessola, Sant'Angela della Polvere*

*Looking over San Giorgio along the Canale della Giudecca, with il Redentore (far left),
la Salute and the start of the Canal Grande*

Left: **The Island of San Servolo**
("The Island of Madness")
Once the official mental asylum of Venice, it is now the Campus for the Venice International University, opened in 1995.

There is also a museum housing equipment from the asylum.

*Right: Part of the **Arsenale**, with the Armstrong Mitchell hydraulic crane (centre) being restored with funds raised by the Venice in Peril Fund (VIPF). (I am a member)*

As you can imagine, I was in my element up here! It was such a glorious late afternoon, there were hardly any people, and I could "snap" away to my heart's content, which I did! I took so many photos that it's been difficult to choose which to include in this book, but I hope you like the ones I eventually picked.

Once down from the Campanile, I spent some time looking at the Biennale exhibition of the Italian artist Michelangelo Pistoletto's "One and One Makes Three" - a series of photographs on glass of Cuban society, a theme dear to my heart. I did enjoy them.

Back in San Marco, whilst walking by Florian's, I saw the entrance to the Procuratie Nuove where I knew I would find the Istrian stone "Winged Figure with Elephant", probably sculpted by Giambattista Albanese (1573-1630), adopted by VIPF for restoration in 2013. It is possibly linked to Victory and Virtue, though this is not certain. Having seen a photo when it was covered in green algae, the restoration is superb. I love it!

My being in the courtyard attracted a bit of attention from the policeman on duty there (this is the Magistrate's Office), but when I explained why I was interested in the little elephant (the only one in Venice as far as I know), the officer said he loved it too and was so grateful it had been "put back together again".   Thanks again VIPF!

By now it was time to head back to the Bel Sito prior to dinner. I gazed longingly at the pastries in Florian's, but walked on by (such willpower). Back at the hotel, I changed and headed off to Le Café, making a detour via San Maurizio again. And (in case you're interested) I had glass of Prosecco, an excellent spaghetti carbonara and (my favourite) a really fattening crêpe with mascarpone, arancia (orange), canella (cinnamon) and lashings of Grand Marnier. Somehow crossing the bridges back home didn't seem quite so painful!!

Sunday 24th September 2017

I opened the shutters. Surely not! The worst Victor Meldrew day possible! It had been beautiful yesterday, but now it was absolutely pouring with rain, cold and windy. I had the morning organized: I was going to St George's Anglican Church for Communion. But the afternoon might pose a bit of a problem. Still, whatever the weather, it wouldn't stop me from getting out and about, even if it wasn't where I wanted to go to originally.

First things first, though. Stock up on breakfast! This morning I shared a table with a French lady, on her own, who had come for the Madame Butterfly opera at La Fenice that afternoon. She spoke no English, so I had to dig deep in those "little grey cells" to resurrect my rusty French. But we got on so well and agreed to meet up later so I could hear how the performance had gone. Time now, though, to put on mac, dig out brolly and brave the elements to head off to St George's in time for the 1030 Communion Service.

The Anglican Church of St George, Campo San Vio

I got there a bit early and, with a few others, got soaked waiting for the doors to open, but once inside everyone was most welcoming. The Service was taken by a lay preacher this morning (the resident Vicar was off travelling somewhere), but he gave an excellent sermon. The congregation numbered about 30 or so: ex-pat residents (sadly Lady Clarke, widow of Sir Ashley Clarke, founder of the VIPF, hadn't come today, because of the weather I think - I had so wanted to meet her), plus Anglicans from the UK, Canada, USA and Australia. There were no coffee facilities, but we were invited to stay for a glass of Prosecco/juice and nibbles, which I did. I had long chats

*The Anglican **Church of St George** (the cream building, left), in the Campo San Vio, next to the Palazzo Barbarigo and near the Gallerie dell'Accademia (photo taken March 2017)*

about my books (which I showed them), rowing and all sorts of topics. They were such a nice group: I learned a lot and much enjoyed the Service and the hospitality afterwards.

A bit about St George's. Briefly, Sir Henry Wotton's embassy from King James 1 to La Serenissima brought the first Anglican Chaplain, Nathaniel Fletcher, to Venice in 1604/5. Anglican Chaplains always accompanied diplomatic missions, both resident and extra-ordinary, until the Republic ended with the invasion by Napoleon in 1797. After the Congress of Vienna, Great Britain established a consulate here in Venice and Anglican services were held regularly by visiting clergy.

In 1842, The Diocese of Gibraltar was established to oversee the permanent chaplaincies and provide clergy for English-speaking communities in the Mediterranean. In 1888 a committee of English residents was formed, with two clergy and the Bishop of Gibraltar, to establish a permanent chaplaincy in Venice, and when the Venezia-Murano Glass and Mosaic Company went bankrupt in 1889, title was obtained to their warehouse building in the Campo San Vio. It was subsequently given to the Diocese as the "English church in Venice" and, apart from 1935-45 during the war years, services have been held here ever since. After 1945 the church became a garrison chapel, with public services

*Inside **St George's Anglican Church**, Campo San Vio, with the Great War Memorial on the left.*

being resumed later for the Summer Season.

There are several beautiful memorial stained glass windows in the church dedicated to people like Robert Browning, John Ruskin, and Sir Ashley Clarke who was Church Warden for more than twenty years and was largely responsible for acquiring the Chaplain's House in Dorsoduro (near the house of Ezzra Pound).

There is also an important Great War memorial inside. And the stunning bronze doors, made from British cannon, one from the Crimean War and one dated 1795, were restored in 2015. I wish I could list all the history, but it is a wonderful church.

September 2017: **St George's**, *Campo San Vio, with the Biennale "The Golden Tower"*
by James Lee Byars

Unfortunately, the whole of Sunday proved to be a complete wash-out! It was still pouring when I came out of St George's, so I sloshed my way down the Fondamenta Bragadin to the Zattere, where I found a little taverna and had a delicious pizza and café latte.

The best thing, I decided, was to vaporetto-hop, so I got on one at Zattere and we sailed down la Canale della Giudecca to Ferrovia, where I caught another one to take me back down the Canal Grande towards San Marco. I had thought I'd get off at San Samuele and visit the Damien Hirst Biennale exhibition "Treasures from the Wreck of the Unbelievable" in the Palazzo Grassi which everyone was raving about (just to broaden my artistic appreciation even though I don't much care for his work: I find it too disturbing). But when I saw the queue of people at the side door, I had a rapid change of heart. I hated his sculpture outside anyway, so I don't think I would have enjoyed the exhibition and would have resented having to pay €18.00 to get in to see something I didn't like!

So, as it had stopped raining at last, I stayed on the vaporetto to San Marco Giardinetti and had a little walk around there for a while, before heading back to the Bel Sito and settling down with cuppa and "Death at La Fenice" till it was time to head for Le Café. . Not an exciting day, but I'd enjoyed just pottering around for a change and taking it easy.

Damien Hirst. *Not for me, I'm afraid! I love the gentleness of Impressionism.*

Monday 25th September 2017

Oh, the vagaries of the weather! Today looked like being a "scorcher", which was just as well as this was my day for going to Pellestrina. I'd sailed passed this island en route to Chioggia on my last trip, but it was so misty I saw little. However, having read Donna Leon's "A Sea of Troubles" which takes place on Pellestrina, I was keen to explore this strip of land for myself.

I caught up with Janine at breakfast and heard all about her visit to the Opera, which she loved. Stocking up then on water and muesli bars (very few eating places on Pellestrina), I headed off to San Zaccaria to begin my journey.

Passage to Pellestrina

It's a bit complicated to get to Pellestrina! Depending on the timings of the public transport, it takes about an hour. First, I had to get to Lido (Santa Maria Elisabetta), the main vaporetto station, where I was to catch the orange No 11 bus, so I boarded a large motonavo at San Zaccaria and set off via Giardini and Sant'Elena. Once at Lido, I

it seemed a good idea to have a "comfort stop" as there is nothing on Pellestrina. Nor on Lido, so it seems – at the beach maybe, but not round here! Come on Venice: this just isn't good enough. You really have to do better!

I waited about ten minutes for the No 11 (then two came at once—what's new?). I got on the first and we set off down the Gran Viale Santa Maria Elisabetta, which I knew fairly well from previous visits. We followed the Adriatic coast, passing the Residenze (Hotel) des Bains, and I was distressed to see that it was in an even worse state than I had seen it before. Apparently, so I found out later, there had been a bad fire a few years ago that had destroyed most of the interior. It was now uninhabitable, and was waiting for some developer to buy and renovate it to its former glory. Hopefully soon!

We continued along Lungomare Gugliemo Marconi, passing the famous Excelsior Hotel, haunt of all the film stars during the International Film Festival in September. Elegance is not the word! And opposite, in complete contrast, is the ultra-modern complex where all the films are shown. On down to Città Giardino, where we turned right onto the main Via Sandro Gallo to Malamocco. Through that little town, then on to Alberoni, until we reached the ferry.

I must say I do like Lido. After the frenzy of Venice, I find the tranquillity and greenness of this island very refreshing. Wherever I looked, all the buildings, apartment blocks, private houses etc seemed to be in pristine condition and it was a delightful journey. Once at the ferry, we were joined by the second bus which had taken another route along the La Laguna side, and both buses drove straight onto the waiting boat.

It only took 15 or so minutes to cross the Lido di Malamocco to Santa Maria del Mare on the other side, and both buses then set off down the long, straight "main" road (*Strada Comunale dei Murazzi)* that follows the Adriatic coast down to Ca'Roman at the other end.   But before I continue with my trip, a bit here about :

Pellestrina

Pellestrina, like Lido, is made up of sandy detritus carried down by rivers flowing into La Laguna, which La Serenissima diverted centuries ago from their estuaries to prevent silting up of the waters around Venice herself. 11 kms long and never more than 200 metres wide, with a beach (devoid of sun umbrellas and souvenir sellers - hurray!) on the Adriatic side, Pellestrina, along with Lido, protects Venice from the Adriatic. In places it is only the width of the Murazzi, narrow Istrian stone dam walls built in 1751 as a series of embankments along its Adriatic side designed to safeguard against acqua alta in Venice and La Laguna. At the southernmost end is Ca'Roman, a protected nature reserve of pine trees, popular with bird watchers, and the Roman fortress of Ca'Roman.

The island is divided into four sestieri (Scarpa, Zennari, Vianelli and Busetti—named after the four major families sent there by the Mayor of Chioggia to re-populate it after it was destroyed during the Veneto-Genoa conflict of 1378-81. Today there are four main villages: San Pietro in Volta, Porto Secco, Sant'Antonio di Pellestrina and Pellestrina itself, with the tiny settlement of Villagio Caroman on the southern end.

The village communities are close-knit, mainly fishermen. The islanders speak Venetian, and most Pellestrinotti appear to be descendants of those original families sent over from Chioggia and so have the surnames Scarpa or Vianello (cf Donna Leon's "A Sea of Troubles"). Of necessity, therefore, nicknames are used to identify everyone!

Though the earth is sandy, there is a small amount of market gardening, but the main sources of revenue on Pellestrina are fishing and bobbin lace-making, made by weaving cotton threads that unroll from *fuselli* (bobbins) on a round cushion (called a *tombolo, balòn* in Venice). Unlike the lace makers in Burano and Torcello, the ladies of Pellestrina use a needle instead. There is also an important vaporetto repair yard.

During the summer months there is some tourism, with a few more B&B's and the odd pizzeria springing up, but the choices are limited and you have to look hard to find them.

*Pellestrina's beach
along her Adriatic side*

The **Strada Comunale dei Murazzi**, *the long, straight, "main" road at the back of the villages which follows the Murazzi (the sea defence walls down to Ca'Roman)*

Most visitors (mainly from Chioggia and Lido) go to Pellestrina just to sample the sea food specialities on offer at the island's two famous restaurants, Da Nane and Da Celeste. Apparently Da Nane in San Pietro di Volta was a particular favourite of French President Mitterrand. However, it would seem the prices at Da Nane and Da Celeste are extortionate (€80.00 per head plus), so personally I'd eat elsewhere! (Not that that is easy— not many bars and cafés around: so best to take some food with you, as I did! Also, a warning: there are no public toilets, as I was to find out!)

With regard to fishing, the most prized sea food are clams (*vongole -"una vongola"* is a clam); and the more highly prized *cappi lunghi (razor clams)*. However, their harvesting has led to much tension and violence between the *vongolari* and other La Laguna fisherman because of the indiscriminate destruction of large expanses of sea bed by the vacuum cleaner like scoops *(over)*. The *vongolari* are perceived as destroying whole colonies of clams and their breeding beds, and are not very popular. In the past the *vongolari* also dredged up their clams on the very limit of the prohibited fishing area at Porto Marghera (in front of the oil refinery), making their catch unsafe to eat. Spot checks and regulations were in place, but who knows where a clam comes from, and money was known to "change hands"!   One hopes that by now the industry has been much "cleaned up" and that stricter controls and regulations are in place.

Left: A clam fishing boat with the scoop at the front

Right: A Pellestrina fisherman's "des res"!

But to continue with my trip.

Because the *Strada Comunale dei Murazzi* runs behind the villages, you can't see them so it's rather difficult to know where to get off the bus. Also, 11 kms is a long way to walk in the heat of the day , so you have to judge it right. I knew I needed to get passed San Pietro in Volta, the first village you come to after the ferry crossing, and then Porto Secco and San Antonio (where there's not that much to see), so I'd end up more or less in the centre of Pellestrina itself. I slightly misjudged it, however, and found myself just outside. Still, at least I was on the island —and in Pellestrina, more or less! I crossed over the road, climbed the Murazzi and had a quick look at the beach. Then, conscious I needed to find a Carizzada (a cross street joining the *Strada Comunale to* the La Laguna side road), I walked on till I found one. As I was to discover, though, they are very few and far between!

At the end of the Carizzada I went into the lovely Chiesa di San Antonio di Padova, where I found an elderly gentleman tying, with some difficulty, gold ribbons on the end of the pews. He very proudly told me it was his 50th wedding anniversary and he and his wife were having a re-dedication service that afternoon. He was obviously so happy and I gave him the most heartfelt congratulations my Italian could manage. I explained that I conducted civil marriage ceremonies and we pondered on how many young couples today would ever reach their 50th. Not many, I fear (one of mine only lasted a fortnight). As he was struggling a bit with the ribbons (arthritis in his hands, he told me), I offered to do the rest, for which he was very grateful. I enjoyed tying them on for him and we chatted away, me not quite understanding it all, but getting the gist of what he was saying. I then wished he and his wife every happiness, and went on my way. Such a happy encounter!

Some gold ribbons already tied on

Pellestrina

*The **Carizzada Via Sandro Getto**, with the Campanile della Chiesa di San Antonio di Padova at the far end*

Pellestrina is really nice: quiet, colourful—a sleepy little fishing village. I sat on the sea wall eating my muesli bar (no sign of anywhere else to eat!), but by now I was conscious that I needed to find a loo! An elderly Scottish couple (I heard the accent) came striding by with their walking poles, obviously seasoned hikers. We exchanged pleasanteries, and I enquired about the toilet situation. "Och no" they said. "There isn't one on Pellestrina, and the nearest (only?) bar is a good half an hour's walk away.

*The village of **Pellestrina**, reminiscent of Burano with its colourful houses*

Excuse the indelicate subject, but this was bad news and not what I wanted to hear! It looked like it might have to be the beach. However, just ahead was a little general store, the only shop I'd seen so far, so I went in hoping that the lady behind the counter might have some ideas on the situation. She was speaking Venetian (hadn't a clue what she was saying) but switched to Italian to talk to me. I explained my predicament and asked for her help! Her best advice was to turn right out of the shop, ring the bell of Signora ?? (didn't catch the name—wouldn't have made any difference if I had), and ask if I could use her loo! OK. So I turned right and was confronted by quite a few houses with door bells? Which one was it? I'd no idea. But then a young Italian couple who had also been in the shop behind me, offered to help. What I needed to do was go back the way I'd just come and after about 10 minutes I'd come to a building and I could use theirs. I must still have looked very puzzled, for they then said they'd take me and off we set, eventually ending up in a doctor's surgery tucked away at the end of what looked like a school building. The waiting room was full, and I got some very funny looks, but by then I really didn't care. I uttered "toilette" and dashed through the first door I saw with a lady on it, hoping that it wasn't a lady doctor's consulting room. It wasn't. Phew!

Much relieved, I continued happily on my way!

By now the school day had ended and the little road was jammed with children on bikes eager to get home . No school bus here!   You almost got mown down in the rush, but I don't blame them. It was a lovely day and I'm sure they had lots of other things to do.

I walked on until I came to the Santuario della Madonna dell'Apparizione *(below)*, the site on which The Virgin Mary is said to have appeared to a young Pellestrina boy, Natalino Scarpa dei Mutti, on 4 August 1716, announcing in Venetian that the Christians would be victorious over the Turks. This event is celebrated on 4 August each year with dances, boat races and a big feast. On the first Sunday of August there is also the traditional Pellestrina boat race, attended by hundreds of rowers from all over Venice. The "in" place to be! I had a quick look inside—beautiful in its simplicity.

By now it was almost 3 o'clock, time to head back to Venice. Next door to the Santuario was Carizzada No 46 (goodness knows where the other 43 were—I only found 3!), so I walked along it to the Strada Comunale to catch the bus back.   I didn't have long to wait and really enjoyed the ferry crossing and ride through Lido back to the vaporetto station. I was so tired, but I'd had a really happy, successful day and had achieved all I had set out to do, so I was pleased.   One more hidden gem to add to the list!

Once back in Venice, I decided now was the only time I had in my "schedule" to take my two sets of books back to Alta Acqua as the owner had said he'd buy them.   I had to force my legs to move and my hip was a real pain, but I struggled on, getting lost in the maze of alleyways around La Merceria (so much for taking the short cut, Gillian!) and viewing each bridge with increasing dismay. When I got to Alta Acqua the owner was resting, but his son was there. He looked at my books, liked them, but said they were not the sort of books they would buy. Seems the man I thought was the owner just worked there, and had no authority to say they would buy them. I can't tell you how despondent I was. I almost cried. Worse still, I had to walk all the way back (oh for a bus or taxi) carrying my heavy books.   It can be so demoralizing sometimes being a [new] author!

When I finally made it back to the Bel Sito, it was suggested I meet the owner of the hotel, a charming lady called Signora Rossella Serafini. She at least was interested in my books! She also asked if I would like to see where she lived—in the hidden Palazzo Marin next door. I readily agreed and so it was arranged we'd meet at 9 o'clock next morning (I had my tour of the Torre dell'Orologio booked for 10 am).

By now I was still feeling exhausted but much happier as I made my way to Le Café. I had worked hard for my glass of Prosecco tonight and deserved it!

Tuesday 26th October 2017

Palazzo Marin, Campo Santa Maria del Giglio

As arranged, I met Signora Serafini at 9 am and off we went to her Palazzo. This truly was a hidden gem. I had no idea it was there, behind big double green doors right next to the hotel!   It was originally occupied by la Contessa Isabella Teotochi (born in Corfu) who had come to Venice in 1836. She had first married Carlo Antonio Marin, then Giuseppe Abrizzi. She was a cultured lady renowned for her beauty, as well as being a scholar, and her soirées attracted such notables as Byron, Goethe and, of course,

Il Palazzo Marin

Casanova to whom she dedicated her biography about his sculptures and patronage of the arts (and who, unsurprisingly, was also her lover for a time!).

Today the Palazzo is the venue for private parties, wedding receptions, gala events, meetings and conventions, cultural events and Chamber music concerts. Signora Serafini occupies only a small part of it. The rear entrance is on the Rio della Fenice and faces the stage door of the opera house. Many of the famous opera singers attend parties there after the performances. La Signora is at present renovating the ground floor, constantly being flooded at acqua alta, but it will look fantastic when it's finished.   As with all Palazzi, the upkeep of such a building is tremendous, but it is so beautiful inside and is so worth preserving, however one does it! My photographs don't do it justice.

I could have stayed there all morning, but Signora Serafini had to get back to the hotel and I had to get to the Museo Correr where I was picking up the tour of the Torre dell'Orologio. I thanked her profusely. It had indeed been a privilege to be invited into Palazzo Marin, one of Venice's "hidden gems" - an important part of Venetian history. I wished her every success with this new venture. I wish it could be one of my venues!

Tour of La Torre dell'Orologio

As I've already covered the history of this Torre d'Orologio (clock tower) in Volume 1 (p. 46-48), I won't go into too many details about it here save that this astronomical clock, similar to the one in Padova, was commissioned by Doge Agostino Barbarigo in 1493 and was built and installed by Gian Paolo and Gian Carlo Rainieri (father and son) from 1496-99. Over the centuries the clock has been subject to many restorations, some controversial. The 1996 restoration should have been carried out by Piaget, the

*La Torre, showing the **Mori** on the top; the winged lion of San Marco; the blue minute and month windows below; the **Madonna** and balcony where the figures appear at Epiphany and during Ascension Week; and the sundial clock face*

watchmakers, but the Venetian authorities instead entrusted the job to Giuseppe Brusa, an historian, and Alberto Gorla, a clock mechanic.   They were subsequently criticised for poor choices, unsound restoration methodology and inappropriate workmanship.

One claim to fame for this beautiful clock is that in the 1979 James Bond film *Moonraker,* Bond ends up throwing the "bad guy" through a model of the glass face of this clock and down onto a piano in the Piazza San Marco. Quite dramatic!

The workings of the clock are fascinating: a bit too technical for me I fear, but from what I understand it's basically weights, chains and pulleys, with a foliot escapement. Hopefully my photos will give you a better idea.

In 1497 the Venetian government paid Rainieri and his family to live in the Torre as "temperatore" (custodian) and keep the clock in good order. Subsequent generations have held that post until 1998, when the position was abolished, the last custodian being Alberto Peratoner, who roundly criticised the 1996 restoration.   Personally, I think the clunks and clicks would have driven me mad, but it was a prestigious position to hold.

The Torre d'Orologio is impressive. It was strategically placed where it could be seen from La Laguna and was intended to symbolise, particularly to visitors, the wealth and glory of Venice. The lower two floors form a large arch into the main street of Venice, La Merceria. Today it is one of 11 historical sites managed by the Fondazione Musei Civici di Venezia.

The tour, booked at the Museo Correr, costs €6.00 and is excellent. Well worth it, in my opinion. But a word of warning: there are a great many stairs to climb, and the last section is up a very narrow iron spiral staircase. As a bell-ringer, I'm used to such stairways, but some people may find it quite challenging.

Left: the Custodian's former lounge!

Right: the original stone weights, now replaced by iron ones

I did say it was technical!

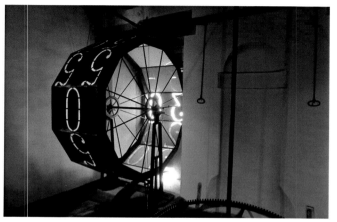

Above left: *The five minute drum which clicks round every 5 minutes There is a month drum the other side)*

Above right: *The clock's machinery (I leave it to you to work it out!)*

Left: *The Magi and Angel that appear at Epiphany and during Ascension Week*

Left: *The beautiful astronomical clock face, showing the signs of the Zodiac and the 24 hours in the day*

(Through which Bond hurled the bad guy in "Moonraker"!)

Right: *The **Mori** (one old, one young) that strike the hours*

(Originally called "the giants", they may have been shepherds because of their sheepskins. Their dark patina gave them their nickname of "i Mori")

By the time the tour ended, it was about 11.30 and my next Tour of La Fenice wasn't due to start until 1.30.   Time for a treat —lunch at Florian's (just a sandwich and a caffe latte—this isn't the establishment in which to go overboard!). It was elegant inside and when I thought of all the personalities who had graced its doors, I did get a certain sense of history and occasion.   No celebrities today, but I enjoyed the experience nevertheless.

Lunch at the Caffée Florian, with orchestra!

Tour of La Fenice ("The Phoenix") Opera House

Wonder of wonders! La Fenice hadn't burned down again before I got to do the tour (see section on La Fenice, Volume 2, p. 86-88)!

Still unlucky in obtaining a ticket for an opera, I'd been looking forward to going on this tour instead.   I'd booked on line about a month before I left for this trip, and managed to get on one for a day when I would be here.   I was all set!

*The entrance to **La Fenice Opera House***

Built in 1792 to replace San Benedetto, Venice's grandest opera house lost through a legal battle with the Venier family to regain control of the ground on which it was built, La Fenice is today a world-renowned opera house, of course, but it has had a somewhat chequered past, including being burned down twice in 1836 and 1996. However, as the name implies, it has risen up from the ashes and is once again the most beautiful of theatres, attracting world class singers and conductors.

Madame Butterfly" (which my French friend at the Bel Sito had said was wonderful) had just ended, and the stagehands were now getting ready for *"La Traviata"* in two weeks

time, so the Rio di Fenice was a hive of activity with topi coming and going with different sets of scenery. This is the only opera house in the world where both cast and scenery have to be transported in by water, so it can be quite challenging at times for the pro-duction team. *(Outside the stage door)*

Inside the world renowned La Fenice Opera House, looking towards the Royal Box

The original La Fenice was designed by Gianntonio Selva, but it did not include a Royal Box. All the boxes were of the same size. However, in 1797 Napoleon invaded La Serenissima , and then handed the Republic over to the Austro-Hungarian empire for eight years. In 1805 Venice reverted back to French rule. The attendance of Napoleon at La Fenice in 1807 necessitated the demolition of three central boxes in the second and third tiers to make way for a "temporary" box befitting his importance, the "Republican House". In 1808 Selva then built a definitive model, later destroyed in the fire of 1836. During the early 1800's many alterations/changes back to the original had to be made during the occupation of the French and Austrians, but with the unification of Italy and Venice's entrance into the Kingdom of Italy, this box then became the official Royal Box . You can see the Italian royal family's insignia inside. It truly is superb.

There are also *Sale Apollinee* — five rooms whose layout today dates from 1937. These rooms are now used during the intervals by the audience occupying the first three tiers of boxes and the stalls. Unlike the rest of the opera house, about a fifth of these rooms survived the 1996 fire, though you can still see some smoke damage.

The Royal Box

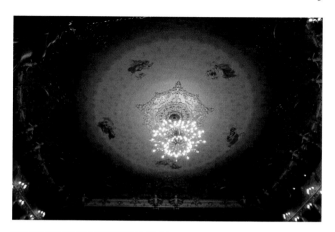

Above : *Changing scenery (sadly, we couldn't see the beautiful dark green fire resistant synthetic velvet curtains decorated with 1100 flowers in gilt leather. Such a pity: they are stunning, I'm told)*

Above right: *The exquisite centre chandelier (the original one was made in Liverpool!)*

Right: *The all-important Bar !*

*The stunning **Sala Grande**, or ballroom, is the main room of the Sale Apollinee. This room was almost completely destroyed in 1996 but has been faithfully restored to its original design. It is now an elegant venue for balls, concerts and important social gatherings.*

Again, I thoroughly enjoyed this tour. There is a small area devoted to Maria Callas as well as an excellent model of the whole opera house. We didn't get to see back stage, of course, as they were very busy with scenery, but even so we walked around a lot, and there was coffee and pastries available in the bar if we wanted them. I do recommend visiting La Fenice. It is a very special place after all.

It was still quite hot when I left the opera house, so I decided a boat trip might be a good way of cooling down. One of the people I had met at St George's Church had told me that you get a good view over La Giudecca and Venice from the Skyline Bar and Terrace at the ex-Mulino Stucky (Hilton hotel), so I got on a vaporetto at San Zaccaria and got off at Redentore to have a look at that church before meandering along the Fondemente San Giacomo, de Ponte Picolo and San Biagio to the hotel.

For me the outline of Il Redentore (one of the five "plague churches") is one of the most imposing in Venice. The interior is impressive also, but I'm afraid my own photo of it is not, so I have taken the liberty of including one taken by *Didier Descouens—Own work* so you can appreciate how beautiful it is, a fitting thanksgiving for the end of the 1576 epidemic of the plague.

*The interior of **La Chiesa del Redentore**, on La Giudecca*

(one of the five "plague churches")

(Photo on this occasion courtesy of Didier Descouens —Own Work)

Having left il Redentore, I enjoyed my stroll along the banks of the Canal della Giudecca till I reached the ex-Mulino Stucky. I'm afraid I got no further than the Lobby of the hotel, however. Non-residents are not allowed on the Skyline terrace until 5 pm, which is quite fair enough. Guests deserve their exclusivity! But if the Lobby is anything to go by, the Skyline must be very nice indeed! I'll try to return—one day!

Strolling along the Fondamenta San Biagio to the ex-Mulino (some maps show Molino) Stucky (now the Hilton Hotel)

The Lobby of the ex-Mulino Stucky (Hilton Hotel)

As it was only 4 o'clock, I didn't feel like hanging about for an hour just to go up on the terrace, so I made my way back to the vaporetto stop at Palanca, crossed over to the Zattere, walked up to Accademia, hopped on another vaporetto to Giglio and arrived back at the Bel Sito at about 5.30 pm. A good time to relax in the courtyard with a very welcome beer for half an hour or so, talking to other guests, before making my way (again!) to Le Café for a delicious chicken salad, my "usual tipple" (glass of Prosecco) and yet another crêpe (chocolate and cream this time)! Another satisfying day!

Wednesday 27th September 2017

One more day before I went home, but as usual I had an itinerary planned. I'm an organised soul!

The weather was beautiful yet again (sorry Victor!) so, after a good breakfast I made my way back to Accademia yet again to search out a particular exhibit which my "founts of all Biennale knowledge"- hairdresser Jon and sculptress wife Anne - had raved about. They did rave about Damien Hirst too, but we agreed to differ on that!

*Venice Biennale 2017: The Pavilion of Humanity - **OBJECTION***

BIENNALE 2017

The Pavilion of Humanity - OBJECTION
(the "B" is reversed in the title)

There is much to write about the concept of this exhibition, so I shall try to précis it as best I can.

It is a collaboration between artists Ekin Onat from Turkey and Michal Cole from Israel, an unusual combination, who together make an argument for compassion and non-violent protest.   Both ladies believe in the power of art to speak the truth on human rights, injustice and inequality.

The exhibition takes place in a private house near the Ponte dell'Accademia. I had seen where it was (it's a red house with a little bridge to it, though you have to go down a tiny calle at the side to enter the house). The artists question the perception of home as a neutral space against oppression, censorship and persecution in everyday life. There are art works in every room which alter the meaning of this familiar setting.   This is a powerful statement by these two ladies, but for me "Top Gun" on the ground floor

The Pavilion of Humanity—*OBJECTION* (*Top Gun*)

is stunning. Michal Cole uses men's ties as a symbol of "masculinity and phallic poten-cy", ie the male is the most important person in a particular sphere, and also the ac-ceptance of a male-dominated civilisation. She has used 25,000 ties (many acquired by herself) and it took her a year and a half to complete the exhibit. This is a most im-pressive exhibition, curated by Gillian Fox and supported by the University of Arts, Lon-don. Both artists are to be congratulated. The message is a powerful one.

After leaving OBJECTION, I caught a vaporetto at Accademia to San Tomá to walk to the Frari. After another look inside, I carried on via winding alleyways till I found the Scuola San Giovanni Evangelista, founded in 1262 as one of the six great lay confraternities, suppressed by Napoleonic Edict in 1807, but later revived and still active today. Now the monumental staircase is in need or urgent conservation as it's pulling away from the back of the building and the 19th century tie-rods are no longer fit for purpose. The VIPF is contributing €15,000 towards supporting the vault below the landing, strength-

ening the brick buttressing and renewing the tie-rods ahead of the main €1 million restoration project which will be done in phases as and when the money is raised. Sadly the Scuola was in use and closed to visitors so I was unable to see the work in progress, but the entrance *(left)* is very imposing.

Time for lunch! I found a little pizzeria tucked away down an alley, had a great pizza and 7-Up and, fortified, headed off for my afternoon's wanderings. As it was still lovely weather, I had decided to devote the afternoon to a trip to the outer islands of Burano and Torcello (via Murano—I wasn't going to stop off there this time) which I had last visited on a freezing, wet March day on 2015. To start my journey, though I had to get to the Fdta Nove to catch the right vaporetto. As I didn't fancy walking all the way, I walked along the Fdta Rio Marin to the Ponte dei Scalzi and hopped on a vaporetto at Ferrovia which would take me via the Canal di Cannaregio to the Fdta Nove stop. There are quite a few landing stages at Fdta Nove, so I had to be careful I picked the right one, or I would otherwise have ended up at Sant'Erasmo or the Punta Sabbioni! The vaporetto was crowded: obviously I wasn't the only one with this idea! But a lot got off at Murano, so it was a little more comfortable. I decided I'd do Burano last (it's only a 10 minute boat ride at most) and so stayed on to Torcello. Well. What a difference a day makes! I was impressed! Obviously places look so much better on a sunny day, but it would seem a lot of money has been spent on this island since I was last there. The slightly run-down houses along the banks of the Rio now look much spruced-up;

Left: Torcello, with the Campanile of the Basilica and Santa Fosca by its side. Burano (with its Campanile just visible) and Mazzorbo are to the right of the channel

Below: What a difference a day makes! March and September. Walking along the Rio to the Basilica

one has been turned into a lovely new restaurant with a children's play garden; there is a smart hotel almost opposite Locanda Cipriani (competition for them!) and the Casa MUseo Andrich (yes, it does have a capital U!) has had a face-lift. The good old Ponte del Diavolo is still the same as, of course, are the Basilica and Santa Fosca. But (a subject close to my heart!), wonder of wonders, there is an even rarer building, more so than the AD 639 Basilica —a "forica publica" c. AD MMXVII (a newly built public loo block!). I nearly died of shock (I'll spare you the photo, but I just had to take one!). There you are Venice—you can do it when you try!

Beautiful lace from Burano on sale on Torcello

Casa MUseo Andrich, with the remains of ancient pillars

La Basilica (Cattedrale) and Campanile di Santa Maria Assunta, Torcello

I did get to go inside the Basilica and Santa Fosca this time. The present Basilica (also known as the Cattedrale della Santa Maria Assunta) dates from 1008, although parts of it like the marble Pulpit are made up of fragments from the first 7th century church. It is an imposing church and the image of the Virgin Mary in the Apse, surrounded by gold mosaic, is considered to be the best in Venice, not just for the beauty of the image as a whole, but for the look of serenity and tenderness on the Virgin's face. At the other end, covering the whole of the west wall, are the Domesday Mosaics, a stunning and highly decorative mosaic detailing the Last Judgement (sadly no photos were allowed).

I like the intimacy of Santa Fosca, though. It was built in the 11th and 12th centuries on a Greek cross design and has an intricate wooden beamed ceiling for the dome.

Inside Santa Fosca, with its wooden beamed dome

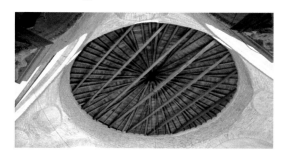

La Chiesa della Santa Fosca, Torcello

I was so enjoying this second visit to Torcello, that I really had to tear myself away, but by now it was nearly 5 o'clock and I still wanted to visit Burano. From what I can remember, my tour in 2015 dropped me off at a landing stage near the main square on the other side of the island to where the main vaporetto stop is now, so it took me a while to get my bearings. I had wanted to go back to that square, but the place was heaving and by now I was quite tired, so I didn't stray too far and just enjoyed the atmosphere and wandering in and out of the shops (even buying an elegant little hand painted ceramic trinket dish!).

It was still such a lovely evening that, again, I was loathe to leave Burano and get back on the vaporetto to Fdta Nove. But the queue for the boat was getting longer and longer by the minute, and as it was gone 6 o'clock, and I still had to catch another vaporetto to take me to the Bel Sito, and I had to pack, "it's now or never" crossed my mind! I managed to squeeze on—just—and we set off on a very bumpy ride for our hour's journey back to Venice, calling at Murano on the way.

Bustling Burano

The start of the promenade near the vaporetto stop on Burano that continues over the bridge to Mazzorbo

En route to Torcello, and back to Burano, I'd been interested to see the development that had taken place on Mazzorbo, the little island to the east of Burano, connected to it by a little footbridge. Before, the little village near the bridge (the only one) had seemed a sleepy backwater. With only one church, Santa Caterina, this island consisted of a few allotments, orchards and gardens, and a playing field in the centre. Now there was a very pleasant promenade stretching from the bridge, yacht moorings and one or two nice looking restaurants. Leaving Burano, we sailed by again, so I had another look. Things are obviously looking up for Mazzorbo as well. When I have more time, I fancy a gentle meander around to see for myself.

It was pretty choppy back to the Fdta Nove, but I found the right landing stage (not easy there!) and joined yet another queue for the vaporetto back to Giglio, via the Canale di Cannaregio. Again another "sardines in a tin" journey, but I eventually arrived at Giglio. Once at the hotel, time for a quick cuppa, throw a few things in my suitcase, and head off for my last meal at Le Café. I'd previously been introduced to the charming owner. Now I met his very nice wife, and they and the other staff made me promise to see them again when I returned. I promised that I would. That will be a real pleasure!

It's not always calm on La Laguna!

Thursday 28th September 2017

As ever, all good things come to an end! My flight didn't leave till 4 pm, so I had the morning to myself for a last minute wander around before catching the 12.01 Alilaguna ferry to the airport.

It was a good flight back (thanks Easyjet!) and again I had great travelling companions sitting next to me.   My taxi was there waiting for me at Gatwick, with the friendly face of one of the drivers I'd been with before, so it was a pleasant drive back. Time now to relax, finish this book, and start planning my next visit. And, as I always say, I will be back!

Ciao Venezia, e come dico sempre—mille grazie!

ACKNOWLEDGEMENTS

Again, I've drawn on many sources for my snippets of information, too many to mention here. I've tried to select information which will be of interest and use and, as I meet and chat with more people on each visit and continue to widen my own knowledge and understanding of this magical city, I hope my enthusiasm is catching on!

But my special thanks go to:

ImprintDigital.com—my faithful and long-suffering printers

Alena Schram, my Canadian author friend, for her support and guidance when I've waivered, doubted myself or been in danger of making a wrong decision!

Vivien Devlin, Guild of Travel Writers, for her sound advice, encouragement, and enthusiasm and belief in my books

Helen Christmas (Cottageweb) for re-designing my website

And, as ever, **my sister Sheila**, who hasn't given up on me quite yet; who, secretly I'm sure, fervently hopes there won't be a Volume 4; but who lives in hope, as I do, that one day I may even be a tiny fraction as popular and successful as Donna Leon!

Disclaimer:

Whilst the author and publisher have made every effort to ensure that the information in this book is correct at time of going to press, the author and publisher do not assume and hereby disclaim any liability to any party for any loss, damage or disruption caused by errors or omissions, whether such errors or omissions result from negligence, accident or any other cause.

INDEX

The Diary of an Awestruck
Traveller Trilogy

The end of the series ....or is it?

The Campanile di San Marco and San Giorgio Maggiore

Tomorrow is another day ......"